ConText

"…rightly handling the word of truth."
2 Timothy 2:15

Elder Jandre Kincannon Sr.

ENTEGRITY
CHOICE PUBLISHING

Entegrity Choice Publishing
PO Box 453 Powder Springs, GA 30127
info@entegritypublishing.com
www.entegritypublishing.com
404.472.9190

Printed in the United States of America

Library of Congress Control Number: 2026908437
ISBN: 979-8-9991668-2-1

I want to dedicate this book to my two sons,
Liam and Jandre Kincannon, Jr., my heart in life form.
I would not be the man I am today without you two.

CONTENTS

INTRODUCTION

Do you ever find reading the Bible a chore? Do you find your-self wrestling with the words "thou, thee, thy, and thine?"

I have been exposed to bad teaching. I want people to have a plan when studying the Bible. I studied the Bible for years to develop my own understanding. I want to help you develop your own understanding. I wrote this book as a guide so that you no longer have to struggle to read or study the Bible or leave with incorrect doctrine.

It is my aim that this book will help you understand the Bible and guide you in your walk with God. It is my desire that you have a clearer understanding of context than you did before reading this book.

"Do your best to present yourself to God as
one approved, a worker who has no need to be
ashamed, rightly handling the word of truth."
2 TIMOTHY 2:15 (ESV)

CHAPTER 1

Keeping Scriptures in Order

CONTEXT (CONTEXT) IS ONE of the biggest advantages to reading any book, let alone the Bible. What does context require? Context requires that I not take a scripture(s) out of context by saying something totally opposite to its true meaning. When reading scriptures, read the entire chapter. Oftentimes, taking the time to read the whole chapter will give you insight into what a particular verse is saying.

For example, Luke 6:38 says, *"Give, and it shall be given unto you; good measure, pressed down, and shaken together, and running over, shall men give into your bosom. For with the same measure that ye mete withal it shall be measured to you again."*

I am sure you have heard this scripture read, particularly at offering time in the church. You may be surprised to know that this scripture has nothing to do with money.

Let's examine this scripture further. In the English Standard Version (ESV), Luke 6:37 has a heading over it that reads

"Judging Others." Luke 6:27 has a heading over it that reads "Love Your Enemies." Luke 6:27 to 6:36 talk about treating others as you treat yourself (paraphrasing).

Luke 6:37 says, *"Judge not, and ye shall not be judged: condemn not, and ye shall not be condemned: forgive, and ye shall be forgiven."* Plainly, the scriptures prior to this verse are not talking about money; they are talking about Christian ethics toward our brother.

Luke 6:37 gives meaning to what Luke 6:38 is saying: *"Give mercy because you never know when you will need it!"* When you read the full chapter, it will break down the verse.

"If you remove the word "text" from the word "context"—you get the word "con"!

Cross-Referencing

THE SECOND METHOD to effectively studying the Bible is cross-referencing. What is that, Preacher? It is where I compare scriptures to see whether they are saying what the Bible says as a whole. I compare them scripture by scripture.

"The Bible has one message, and it does not contradict itself." I say people only make that statement when they are being lazy in studying the word.

I do not use commentaries because I believe they are men's opinions, which could be wrong; however, I salute the scholars who did an enormous amount of work researching and publishing those commentaries. I compare scripture by scripture. Let's look at an example.

A scripture that you have no doubt heard many times is Revelation 3:15–16. This scripture says, *"I know thy works, that thou art neither cold nor hot: I would thou wert cold or hot. So then because thou art lukewarm, and neither cold nor hot, I will spue thee out of my mouth."*

I have often heard people interpret this scripture to mean that cold is the devil and hot is God. That is an incorrect interpretation of that scripture.

First, Jesus says, "I wish." He would not say "I wish" if anything in the scripture was referring to the enemy! Jesus was referring to Laodicean people. Hot has a purpose and cold has a purpose; however, "lukewarm" does not have any purpose! Jesus is saying, "Be purposeful," which agrees with other scriptures.

> *"And we know that for those who love God*
> *all things work together for good, for those*
> *who are called according to his purpose."*
> ROMANS 8:28

Matthew 6:9–13 teaches us how we should pray.

> *"Our Father in heaven,*
> *hallowed be your name,*
>
> *Your kingdom come,*
> *your will be done,*
> *on earth as it is in heaven.*
>
> *Give us this day our daily bread.*
> *And forgive us our debts,*
> *as we also have forgiven our debtors.*

And lead us not into temptation,
but deliver us from evil one."

Being purposeful is consistent with scripture. Jesus wants us to be purposeful. Do you feel you been purposeful for Jesus?

CHAPTER 3

Bible Resources

Find a good version of the Bible that is easy to read. I personally use the English Standard Version (ESV); however, that may not be the version that is an easy read for you. I recommend getting a good study Bible, either paperback or hardcover.

WORD-FOR-WORD BIBLES

These Bible versions aim to remain as faithful as possible to the original Hebrew, Aramaic, and Greek manuscripts, making them ideal for serious biblical study and understanding.

NASB	New American Standard Bible
KJV	King James Version
ESV	English Standard Version
RSV	Revised Standard Version
NKJV	New King James Version

THOUGHT-FOR-THOUGHT BIBLE

These are straightforward translations of the Bible, translated directly from the original Hebrew, Aramaic, and Greek texts.

HCSB	Holman Christian Standard Bible
NRSV	New Revised Standard Version
NAB	New American Bible
NJB	New Jerusalem Bible
NIV	New International Version
TNIV	Today's New International Version
NCV	New Century Version
NLT	New Living Translation

PARAPHRASED BIBLE

There are easy to read, with explained words and shorter sentences creating a clear and simple modern translation. They attempt to translate the ideas from one language to another and are less concerned about using the exact words of the original.

AMP	Amplified Bible
NIRV	New International Reader's Version
GNT	Good News Translation (Good News Bible)
CEV	Contemporary English Version
TLB	The Living Bible
MSG	The Message Bible

Get a good Bible study app. I personally recommend Logos, an awesome app to use.

LOGOS BIBLE APP

Logos is a comprehensive tool for deep, serious study, offering theological libraries and 24/7 research assistance.

YOUVERSION BIBLE APP

YouVersion is known for thousands of versions, audio Bibles, and sharing features.

OLIVE TREE BIBLE APP

Olive Tree is highly rated for its powerful study center, linking Bibles with maps and dictionaries for in-depth research.

BIBLE PROJECT

Bible Project features videos, podcasts, and study notes that explain the Bible's narrative structure

BLUE LETTER BIBLE

Blue Letter Bible is known for providing access to original language tools and concordances.

THROUGH THE WORD (TTW)

TTW offers audio guides for every chapter of the Bible. The guides are designed for daily, understandable study.

Last, find a home church that teaches the Bible from Genesis to Revelation. Connecting with a church will help you grow in your faith.

CHAPTER 4

Bible Knowledge

IN LATER CHAPTERS I will dive into the meat and potatoes, but I want to start with the foundation. Not everyone has the foundation of standard biblical knowledge.

Old Testament Books of the Bible and Authors

Genesis	Moses
Exodus	Moses
Leviticus	Moses
Numbers	Moses
Deuteronomy	Moses
Joshua	Joshua
Judges	Samuel
Ruth	Samuel
1 Samuel	Samuel, Gad, Nathan
2 Samuel	Gad, Nathan
1 Kings	Jeremiah

2 Kings	Jeremiah
1 Chronicles	Ezra
2 Chronicles	Ezra
Ezra	Ezra
Nehemiah	Nehemiah
Esther	Mordecai
Job	Moses
Psalms	David and others
Proverbs	Solomon, Agur, Lemuel
Ecclesiastes	Solomon
Songs of Solomon	Solomon
Isaiah	Isaiah
Jeremiah	Jeremiah
Lamentations	Jeremiah
Ezekiel	Ezekiel
Daniel	Daniel
Hosea	Hosea

Old Testament Books of the Bible and Authors

Joel	Joel
Amos	Amos
Obadiah	Obadiah
Jonah	Jonah
Micah	Micah
Nahum	Nahum
Habakkuk	Habakkuk
Zephaniah	Zephaniah
Haggai	Haggai

Zechariah   Zechariah

Malachi   Malachi

New Testament Books of the Bible and Authors

Matthew	Matthew
Mark	Mark
Luke	Luke
John	Apostle John
Acts	Luke
Romans	Paul
1 Corinthians	Paul
2 Corinthians	Paul
Galatians	Paul
Ephesians	Paul
Philippians	Paul
Colossians	Paul
1 Thessalonians	Paul
2 Thessalonians	Paul
1 Timothy	Paul
2 Timothy	Paul
Titus	Paul
Philemon	Paul
Hebrews	Unknown
James	James (Brother of Jesus)

New Testament Books of the Bible and Authors

| 1 Peter | Peter |
| 2 Peter | Peter |

1 John	Apostle John
2 John	Apostle John
3 John	Apostle John
Jude	Jude (Brother of Jesus)
Revelation	Apostle John

Bible Facts and Statistics

Number of Books in the Bible: 66

Number of Chapters: 1,189

Number of Verses: 31,101

Number of Words: 783,137

Number of Letters: 3,116,480

Number of Promises in the Bible: 1,260

Number of Commands: 6,468

Number of Predictions: Over 8,000

Number of Fulfilled Prophecies: 3,268 verses

Number of Unfulfilled Prophecies: 3,140

Number of Questions: 3,294

Longest Name: Mahershalalhashbaz (Isaiah 8:1)

Longest Verse: Esther 8:9 (78 words)

Shortest Verse: John 11:35 (2 words: "Jesus wept."

Middle Books: Micah and Nahum

Middle Chapter: Psalm 117

Shortest Chapter (by number of words): Psalm 117 (by number of words)

Longest Book: Psalms (150 Chapters)

Shortest Book (by number of words): 3 John

Longest Chapter: Psalm 119 (176 verses)

Number of Times the Word *"God"* appears: 3,358

Number of Times the Word *"Lord"* appears: 7,736

Number of different authors: 40

Number of Languages the Bible Has Been Translated
Into: over 1,200

Old Testament Statistics

Number of Books	39
Number of Chapters	929
Number of Verses	23,114
Number of Words	602,585
Number of Letters	2,278,100
Middle Book	Proverbs
Middle Chapter	Job 20
Middle Verses	2 Chronicles 20:17-18
Smallest Book	Obadiah
Shortest Verse	1 Chronicles 1:25
Longest Verse	Esther 8:9 (78 words)
Longest Chapter	Psalms 119

New Testament Statistics

Number of Books	27
Number of Chapters	260
Number of Verses	7,957
Number of Words	180,552
Number of Letters	838,380
Middle Book	2 Thessalonians
Middle Chapters	Romans 8, 9
Middle Verse	Acts 27:17
Smallest Book	3 John

Shortest Verse   John 11:35
Longest Verse   Revelation 20:4 (68 words)
Longest Chapter   Luke 1

There are 8,674 different Hebrew words in the Bible, 5,624 different Greek words, and 12,143 different English words (King James Version).

The Bible was written by approximately 40 authors over a period of 1,600 years.

The Bible was written over 40 generations in three languages: Hebrew, Greek, and Aramaic.

The Bible was written on three continents, Europe, Asia, and Africa, and in various locations, wilderness, dungeon, palace, prison, in exile, and at home.

The Bible was written by men from various occupations: kings, peasants, doctors, fishermen, tax collectors, scholars, etc.

The Bible was written in various times—war, peace, poverty, prosperity, freedom, and slavery—and in different moods—from the heights of joy to the depths of despair. The Bible was written in harmonious agreement on a widely diverse range of subjects and doctrines.

The Ten Longest Books in the Bible

Psalms   150 Chapters, 2,461 verses, 43,743 words
Jeremiah   52 chapters, 1,364 verses, 42,659 words
Ezekiel   48 chapters, 1,273 verses, 39,407 words
Genesis   50 chapters, 1,533 verses, 38,267 words
Isaiah   66 chapters, 1,292 verses, 37,044 words
Numbers   36 chapters, 1,288 verses, 32,902 words

Exodus	40 chapters, 1,213 verses, 32.602 words
Deuteronomy	34 chapters, 959 verses, 28,461 words
2 Chronicles	36 chapters, 822 verses, 26,074 words
Luke	24 chapters, 1,151 verses, 25,944 words

The Ten Shortest Books in the Bible

3 John	1 chapter, 14 verses, 299 words
2 John	1 chapter, 13 verses, 303 words
Philemon	1 chapter, bb 25 verses, 445 words
Jude	1 chapter, 25 verses, 613 words
Obadiah	1 chapter, 21 verses, 670 words
Titus	3 chapters, 46 verses, 921 words
2 Thessalonians	3 chapters, 47 verses, 1,042 words
Haggai	2 chapters, 38 verses, 1,131 words
Nahum	3 chapters, 47 verses, 1,285 words
Jonah	4 chapters, 48 verses, 1,321 words

This chapter is a good starting point to learn the basic facts of the Bible.

CHAPTER 5

Jimmie
and Cindy

JIMMIE GREW UP in a two-parent household. When he was thirteen, his parents separated and got a divorce; Jimmie was hurt. Although his mom and dad maintained a great relationship, Jimmie had to live in two separate households. Jimmie's dad had primary custody with Mom getting weekends and holidays. His dad was a deacon in the church, so Jimmie knew nothing but church.

Cindy's parents were married. She grew up in one household with both parents. Cindy did not go to church because her parents were atheists.

Cindy and Jimmie met in college and started dating. They shared the same interests.

Jimmie was determined to find a local church while away at college. After weeks of Jimmy and Cindy praying and seeking a church, a mutual friend recommended a church that they decided to visit.

Jimmie fell in love with the church immediately. Cindy told Jimmie that she thought the pastor was nice and the church members very welcoming.

At the end of the service, the pastor introduced himself to Cindy and Jimmie. They told the pastor that they were in college and other relevant details of their lives. Because they had enjoyed the experience and felt good about the church, they returned the following Sunday. During their second visit to the church, the pastor called them forward and began to pray and prophesy to them.

The Bible Is the Final Authority

THE BIBLE HAS to be your final authority. What I mean by this statement is this: If it is not in the Bible, we cannot say it, let alone believe it!

A few years ago, my mom and I decided to go to Atlanta to visit my brother. During my vacation I engaged in several debates about the Bible. Often people say things that are not in the Bible and are misleading people!

While on vacation in Atlanta, a pastor told me that Paul had a wife. I told him that Paul was not married. There is nowhere in scripture that alludes to such a marriage. I told him to prove it to me in scripture, and he couldn't.

If someone cannot show you in scripture what they are telling you, end the conversation. There is nothing more to talk about. Paul was not married. He says, *"I wish you would be single like me."* (1 Corinthians 7:7–8)

My mom agreed with the pastor. They were taught Paul was in the Sanhedrin court, but that is not the case. Paul never references that when he lists his accomplishments. I feel that my mom is a Bible genius. Few people know the Bible better than she does, but she was a victim of bad teaching. That is a hard concept for some to grasp; however, the Bible is the final authority.

I met a lady who put her experiences over scripture! She would experience something that was completely against the Bible or do something that was contrary to what the Bible says, and she used her experiences as gospel. NO! Experience does not supersede scripture.

We have to teach the Bible and the Bible ONLY!

CHAPTER 7

Prophecy

IN CHAPTER 5, the pastor prophesied to Jimmie and Cindy. I want to start by saying that prophecy is in scripture although I think that today's prophets are not like biblical prophets. I will elaborate.

Have you ever felt embarrassed by a prophecy? Did the prophecy feel more like the person was throwing something out based on something they heard? Have you ever been prophesied to and never got what was in said prophecy? Have you ever been prophesied to?

Perhaps you may have experienced one such prophecy. A lot of times people prophesy things that are not God's word, and the person on the receiving end is hurt when God does not honor the prophecy.

God does not do anything outside of His written word. God's written word is the only example we have. His word does not change.

Old Testament prophets called out behavior, especially behavior that displeased God. I am married. If I am mean to my wife and my pastor says, "Hey, Jandre, you should love your wife like Christ loves the church," that's a prophecy. That is biblical and it's a correction of my behavior.

Can God bless a person with a house or car? Yes, can, but that is a prophecy that God may not honor; it's not in His written word. You need to know that you have the right to say you have not received a prophecy. I encourage you to judge everything by God's word, including prophecy.

Be careful when someone comes to you and says they have a word from the Lord for you. If it is truly a word from the Lord, you will not be disappointed! Have you had a false prophecy that ruined your life?

If you have received a false prophecy, I pray that God will remove those words from your heart and mind. I pray God will put you in contact with the right people.

CHAPTER 8

Jimmie Seeks Prayer for His Dad

JIMMIE IS A YEAR INTO COLLEGE. Right before he left for college, he found out his dad had cancer. Jimmie has been faithful about checking on his dad and taking care of him when he has a break from school.

Dad was a cancer survivor before Jimmie was born. He was diagnosed with cancer and God blessed him to beat it. Jimmie has seen healing in a church. He was amazed and hopeful that he could get his dad in church to be healed; however, his dad was too weak to travel.

Jimmie mentioned his dad to the pastor, who started praying. The pastor said to Jimmie, "God is healing his cancer now! God told me that your dad will be healed." Jimmie started crying and praising God. Jimmie called his dad and told him about the words from the pastor about his healing. In a very faint voice his dad said, "Praise God."

The next morning, Cindy received a call from Jimmie's mom. She told her that Jimmie's father had died. Jimmie was in disbelief.

CHAPTER 9

Healing

I WANT TO PITCH my tent right here in this chapter. There have been people who have received prophecies from a so-called prophet or preacher that God will heal their loved ones, and when the healing did not occur, it caused the people pain, hurt, and disappointment. On occasion, some have even left the church.

When a person speaks of healing, they use Isaiah 53:5, which says, *"But he was wounded for our transgressions, he was bruised for our iniquities: the chastisement of our peace was upon him; and with his stripes we are healed."* Let's take a look at this scripture.

This scripture is not talking about physical healing; this scripture is talking about spiritual healing. In context, *wounded for our transgression* is a reference to sin, *our iniquities* is sin, and *by his stripe* is his death; we are healed, saved.

Isaiah 53:6 says, "*All we like sheep have gone astray; we have turned—every one—to his own way; and the Lord has laid on him the iniquity of us all.*" This scripture is talking about the spiritual; it has absolutely nothing to do with physical healing. We are human and have a mortal body; we are made to die.

> "*Then shall the dust return to the earth as it was: and the spirit shall return unto God who gave it.*"
>
> ECCLESIASTES 12:7

We are not made to live forever. Our bodies can get sick, and some sicknesses will take us to our grave. God does not heal everyone; He can, but He doesn't.

I have five points I want to make about healing.

1 God has the power to heal

God does have the power to heal. There is nothing too hard for Him.

> "*If you will diligently listen to the voice of the Lord your God, and do that which is right in his eyes, and give ear to his commandments and keep all his statutes, I will put none of the diseases on you that I put on the Egyptians, for I am the Lord, your healer.*"
>
> EXODUS 15:26

"Jesus Christ the same yesterday, and today, and forever."
HEBREWS 13:8

2 When someone is sick, we should pray for God's will to be done.

Frequently, when believers hear of someone who is sick, they are quick to say, "God is going to heal you." Habitually, you will find that the person was speaking from their emotions rather than relaying what the Lord really said about the sickness. This is why people are hurt and bewildered when a sick loved one is promised healing but quickly dies. We should pray for God's will to be done. It may not be God's will for that person to be healed. Pray God's will!

"And it came to pass, that the father of
Publius lay sick of a fever and of a bloody
flux: to whom Paul entered in, and prayed,
and laid his hands on him, and healed him."
ACTS 28:8

"Wherefore I beseech you that ye would
confirm your love toward him."
2 CORINTHIANS 2:8

3 God sometimes chooses to use sickness for His glory.

In John Chapter 9 we find the miracle of a blind man, when Jesus confesses that this man's sickness is for His glory.

> *"And as Jesus passed by, he saw a man which*
> *was blind from his birth. And his disciples*
> *asked him, saying, Master, who did sin,*
> *this man, or his parents, that he was born*
> *blind? Jesus answered, Neither hath this man*
> *sinned, nor his parents: but that the works*
> *of God should be made manifest in him."*
>
> JOHN 9:1–3

The Apostle Paul had a "thorn in his flesh." God did not heal Paul but used his sickness for His glory. The doctors were constantly amazed at my grandma, Hazel Frederick, who had diabetes for 40 years. God used her sickness for His glory.

4 God did not heal everyone on the earth.

Now Elisha was fallen sick of his sickness whereof he died. And Joash the king of Israel came down unto him, and wept over his face, and said, O my father, my father, the chariot of Israel, and the horsemen thereof. And Elisha said unto him, Take bow and arrows. And he took unto him bow and arrows. And he said to the king of Israel, Put thine hand upon the bow. And he put his hand upon it: and Elisha put his hands upon the king's hands. And he said, Open the window eastward. And he opened it. Then Elisha said, Shoot. And he shot. And he said, The arrow of the Lord's deliverance, and the arrow of deliverance from Syria: for thou shalt smite the Syrians in Aphek, till thou have consumed them. And he said, Take the arrows. And he took them. And he said unto the king of Israel, Smite upon the ground. And he smote thrice, and stayed. And the man of God was wroth with him, and said, Thou shouldest have smitten five or six times; then hadst thou smitten Syria till thou hadst consumed it: whereas now thou shalt smite Syria but thrice. And Elisha died, and they buried him. And the bands of the Moabites invaded the land at the coming in of the year.

2 KINGS 13:14–20

God does not heal everyone. As I stated earlier, we are meant to die. We do not live forever; we cannot see God in this flesh; we have to die.

5 Most times, healing in the Bible is not person-specific but about spiritual healing.

"All we like sheep have gone astray; we have turned every one to his own way; and the Lord hath laid on him the iniquity of us all."

ISAIAH 53:6

As I mentioned earlier, this scripture is talking about spiritual healing and not physical healing. Most instances in scripture, unless they are person-specific, are talking about spiritual healing and not physical.

Everyone has access to spiritual healing, which is salvation, but everyone may not receive physical healing.

I pray that God will heal anyone reading this book who was told that a sick loved one was going to be healed and did not receive healing. That was not God; that was a person who misrepresented God.

CHAPTER 10

Hearing God's Voice

IN CHAPTER 8, the pastor told Jimmie, "God said, 'Your dad will be healed.'" The two most dangerous words are "God said." I want to take time to walk through this chapter.

I do not believe in extra-biblical revelation. What is that preacher? Extra-biblical revelation is anything that is outside of God's word. We in the flesh are subject to human error when we say God spoke to us audibly. Be careful of those people who say God told them everything. For example, someone might say, "God told to me to go to Chick-Fil-A." God does not care about us having a chicken sandwich. Or perhaps there are people who have all the details of your life because supposedly God told them. Stay away from those people. That is what I call extra-biblical revelation: saying God said something that is not in His written word.

*"Do not add to what I command you and do
not subtract from it but keep the commands
of the Lord your God that I give you."*
DEUTERONOMY 4:2 (NIV)

God is not giving any extra-biblical revelation. Everything God had to say He put in the sixty-six books of the Bible.

*"My sheep hear my voice, and I know
them, and they follow me:"*
JOHN 10:27

Today, the number one question asked is, "How do I know God's voice?" Jesus said that His sheep know His voice, but people often ask, "How can I be sure that God spoke to me audibly?" You cannot be sure as long as we are in the flesh. We have emotions, thoughts, and feelings that can cause us to miss what we supposedly heard God say. No one can ever state what God said for sure unless it is in His written word.

Let's break down why Jesus spoke those words in John 10:27. Jesus was talking about His written word when He said, "My sheep know my voice and they follow me." For example, if I am mean to my wife and the Holy Spirit condemns me for how I treated her, then I know that is God because His word says, "Love your wife as Christ loves the church!"

My mom, Kathy Frederick says, "We know what a carnal judge says because they give out written orders." God is a God of order; we have made God appear to fly by the seat of His pants because we lack order. If He were not a God of order, He would have made man first, then the earth.

You may say to the preacher, "How can I find a wife or husband? The word does not specifically state my spouse." Answer these questions: Do they meet your standards that you been praying for in a spouse? Are they willing to make scripture their final authority? Can you align your life with the scriptures and see God? If someone wants to have sex before marriage, God's word says no sex before marriage. When marrying, you should always judge someone based on the scriptures in the love chapter, 1 Corinthians 13.

> *"Love is patient, love is kind. It does not envy,*
> *it does not boast, it is not proud. It does not*
> *dishonor others, it is not self-seeking, it is not*
> *easily angered, it keeps no record of wrongs.*
> *Love does not delight in evil but rejoices*
> *with the truth. It always protects, always*
> *trusts, always hopes, always perseveres."*
> 1 CORINTHIANS 13:4–7 (NIV)

Stay away from people who feel they always hear the word from God or say, "The Lord said . . . " God is not talking as much as people say. He has already spoken through His word.

Avoid those who have extra-biblical revelations. Some time ago, a friend of the family told me that he asked God, "How much do you love me?" He said God began to choke him. I instantly started laughing because the Bible states that God is a loving Father. I told the guy that it was not God. This is another example of why extra-biblical revelations are not of God. The Bible tells us how much God loves us.

> *"For God so loved the world, that he gave his*
> *only begotten Son, that whosoever believeth in*
> *him should not perish, but have everlasting life."*
>
> JOHN 3:16

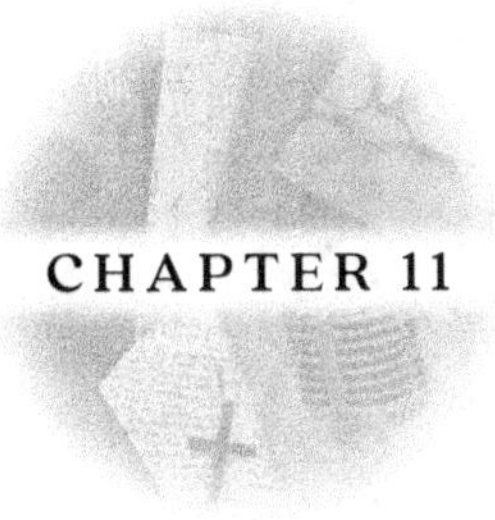

CHAPTER 11

The Funeral

JIMMIE WAS GRIEF-STRICKEN by the passing of his father. It felt unreal to lay his father to rest.

Cindy was right by his side every step of the way.

As Jimmie was getting ready to lay his father to rest, he was asked to speak at his father's funeral. Jimmie got up and said he believed that his father was watching over him.

Jimmie's remarks were based on Hebrews 12:1, which says, *"Wherefore seeing we also are compassed about with so great a cloud of witnesses, let us lay aside every weight, and the sin which doth so easily beset us, and let us run with patience the race that is set before us."*

CHAPTER 12

A Great Cloud of Witnesses

"Wherefore seeing we also are compassed about with so great a cloud of witnesses, let us lay aside every weight, and the sin which doth so easily beset us, and let us run with patience the race that is set before us, Looking unto Jesus the author and finisher of our faith; who for the joy that was set before him endured the cross, despising the shame, and is set down at the right hand of the throne of God."

HEBREWS 12:1–2

Jimmie believed that his father was watching over him. Let's dig into this scripture to divine its meaning.

Personally, I do not believe anyone who has died has any knowledge of what goes on on earth. There is nowhere in scripture that states that the dead know what is happening on earth.

There is nowhere in scripture that says there are angels watching over us. That is not correct, nor do they have any influence on what goes on in the earth.

As I stated in a previous chapter, emotions comfort us but are not biblical. We have to remove our emotions when it comes to scripture because emotions can lead us somewhere from which it may take years to return. Instead of looking at this like we are in a stadium being cheered on by a diseased loved one, let's look at it as a museum where we can read about the works of great pioneers.

How can we read about them? In the Bible. Who are the great faith pioneers? Moses, Abraham, and David, to name a few, can be studied for encouragement. This is what Hebrews 12:1 means. It is attached to what Chapter 11 is saying.

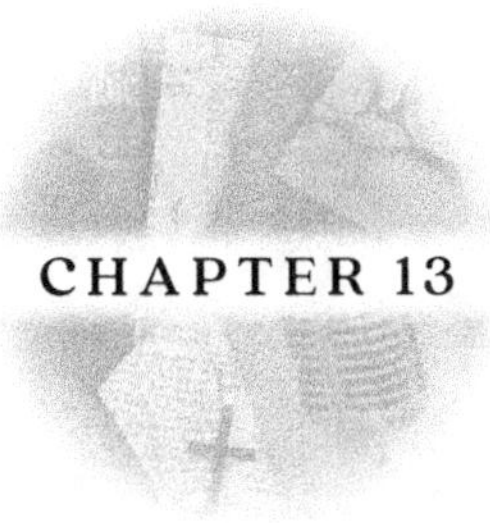

They Got Married

A FEW YEARS AFTER Jimmie's dad's funeral, Jimmie and Cindy finished college. They decided to go to a new church after Jimmie accepted his call to preaching. Jimmie and Cindy decided to tie the knot. They loved each other and believed God had put them together. Cindy stated at the reception that she had manifested Jimmie; she spoke him into existence, and God honored her request.

CHAPTER 14

Manifesting

THERE ARE SOME CHRISTIANS who believe in manifesting. That simply means that you speak something over a long enough time, with enough faith, and God will act and grant you what you desire. I disagree with this belief. God is not a genie. He does not just grant requests at our beck and call.

When we first started to date, my wife had friends who said she manifested me. I pushed back on that statement. I believe it was God's time and will. Words cannot change God's will regardless of how many times you speak them. If it is not meant for you to be married, no matter how many times you say it, it will not happen! Often people say that the Bible says we can call those things that be not as though they were not; that's not what the scripture says.

"As it is written, I have made thee a father of many nations, before him whom he believed,

even God, who quickeneth the dead, and calleth
those things which be not as though they were."
ROMANS 4:17

It is God who calls those things that be not as though they were, not us. I think we as Christians have put so much stock in our words that we get unreal with them and wonder why God is not responding.

Proverbs 18:21 says, *"Death and life is in the power of the tongue."* For example, I believe this scripture is saying that if my wife comes to me with an idea and I say, "Babe, are you trying this again?" my words just hurt her feelings. Instead, I should say, "It is a wonderful idea. If I can be of assistance, let me know." These words will give her life. I do not think this scripture is literally about life and death.

We should be careful with our words. We should be intentional with our words, especially in prayer; however, we should be realistic with our words as well. One thing that amazes me is a person who is sneezing and coughing, and you may ask, "Do you have a cold?" They respond by saying, "No, I am healed." Really? That is foolishness. This is where I reiterate that we have taken that manifest thing too far. It is okay to admit that you have a cold.

I reiterate, no matter how many times you speak it, if it is not in God's will or timing, it is not going to happen. We should never use our words as if God were a genie and has to respond to them; we will be disappointed.

If you are reading this and are not married and have standards, make your petition known to God and tell God, "I am waiting on you, Lord!"

CHAPTER 15

Closing

I WANT TO ENCOURAGE you to make the Bible your final authority!

Get in His word and study.

Take some of the things you have learned in this book, and apply them to your study!

I encourage you to join a Bible-believing and -teaching church!

Find a version of the Bible that you understand. A good study Bible will not help if you cannot understand what it is saying.

As I mentioned before, I love ESV; however you may find the NIV works best for you.

"The beginning of wisdom is this:
Get wisdom, and whatever you get, get insight."
PROVERBS 4:7

I hope I was able to help you with your walk with God.

CHAPTER 16

Hazel K. Frederick

GRANDMA HAZEL K. FREDERICK passed in 2024. My grand-mother was an inspiration to me when it came to the Bible. She would study the Bible for hours and ask me questions about the Bible, which made me study it.

She knew the Bible inside and out. I would not be the Bible scholar I am if it had not been for her guidance. I praise God for her life and light. God kept her many years through her diabetes. She was my example of how good God is! Continue to rest in Jesus, Grandma.

ABOUT THE AUTHOR

ELDER JANDRE KINCANNON, SR. was born in Buffalo, New York. He was called to the ministry and ordained as an elder in 2016. Jandre is a proud scholar of the Bible and has a strong desire to see everyone rightly desire the word of God. He is a proud husband and father of two. He loves the Bible. One of his infamous sayings is "If you take the text out of context, you get con!"

P.O. Box 453
Powder Springs, Georgia 30127
www.entegritypublishing.com
info@entegritypublishing.com
404.472.9190

www.ingramcontent.com/pod-product-compliance
Lightning Source LLC
Chambersburg PA
CBHW072114150726
47999CB00005B/2017